Pushing Isn't Funny
What to Do About Physical Bullying

by Melissa Higgins   pictures by Simone Shin

PICTURE WINDOW BOOKS
a capstone imprint

Note to Parents and Educators

Bullying is a serious problem that many children experience. Physical bullying includes hitting, tripping, kicking, spitting, and hair pulling. It also includes the destruction of personal property, stealing, and physical threats. Children who are physically bullied can experience anxiety, depression, and physical and social problems. Stopping the bullying requires that both kids and adults learn to recognize and deal with bullying quickly and fairly.

This book is intended for an adult to read with a child. While reading, encourage the child to volunteer his or her own experiences about a time when he or she was physically bullied, acted as a bully, or saw physical bullying taking place. Use the text and illustrations as a jumping-off point for conversation and problem solving. For example, what does the child think about Bailey's situation and the advice Bailey is given? What ideas does the child have for dealing with a bully?

Thanks to our adviser for her expertise, research, and advice:
Dorothy L. Espelage, PhD
Department of Educational Psychology
University of Illinois, Urbana-Champaign

Editor: Michelle Hasselius
Designer: Lori Bye
Creative Director: Nathan Gassman
Production Specialist: Laura Manthe
The illustrations in this book were created digitally.

Picture Window Books are published by Capstone,
1710 Roe Crest Drive, North Mankato, Minnesota 56003
www.capstonepub.com

Design elements: Shutterstock:JungleOutThere

Library of Congress Cataloging-in-Publication Data
Higgins, Melissa, 1953–
Pushing isn't funny : what to do about physical bullying / by Melissa Higgins.
pages cm. — (Picture Window Books. No more bullies.)
Audience: K to Grade 3.
ISBN 978-1-4795-6941-0 (library binding)
ISBN 978-1-4795-6957-1 (paperback)
ISBN 978-1-4795-6961-8 (eBook PDF)
1. Bullying—Juvenile literature. 2. Bullying—Prevention—Juvenile literature. I. Title.
BF637.B85H54 2016
302.34'3—dc23   2014049181

Printed in the United States of America
in North Mankato, Minnesota.
032015   008823CGF15

My class is mostly OK. Mrs. Simms, my teacher, is nice. Some of the kids are nice too.

I used to like mornings. That's when we do math, my favorite subject.

But for the past few weeks, I've been having trouble paying attention.

The lunch bell rings, and everyone leaves.
I stay in my seat, my stomach twisting in knots.

"Bailey?" Mrs. Simms says when she sees I'm still there.
"Did you hear the bell?"

I hate lunch period and don't want to go. But I say, **"Yes,"** and shuffle slowly down the hallway.

Footsteps scrape behind me. I hold my breath.

"**Hey, stupid.**" Kim shoves me in the back. "**You're late.**"

I keep moving, hoping Kim will leave me alone.

Then one of Kim's friends steps in front of me, and I have to stop. I start to cry. I don't want to, but I'm scared.

Kim grips my arm tight and twists me around.

"Aw! What's wrong, baby?" Kim says. **"Do you want your mommy?"**

Physical bullying often happens in places that aren't closely supervised, such as bathrooms, hallways, the playground, and the school bus.

"**Stop it!**" I scream. "**Leave me alone!**" I try to pull away, but Kim punches me in the stomach and takes my lunch box.

I fall, gasping for breath and crying even louder.

I spend the rest of lunch period alone on a bench.

Physical bullying can include hitting, pushing, kicking, tripping, slapping, spitting, and hair pulling. It can include stealing and harming personal belongings. Threatening to hurt someone is also bullying.

By the time I get home, I haven't eaten all day. I grab an apple and some cookies.

"Hey, save room for dinner," Mom says. "Didn't you eat lunch?"

"No. I ... I lost my lunch box," I say.

During my bath I try to hide my arm from her.

That night Mom sits with me in my room. "Bailey," she says, "I see your arm is bruised. And this isn't the first time you've lost your lunch box. When I was your age, some kids would push me. Has that ever happened to you?"

I'm embarrassed. Will Mom blame me for being bullied? Will she believe me? And I don't want to tattle. What if Kim finds out and things get worse?

But I really need help, so I tell her about Kim.

Mom listens. Then she asks me to describe what Kim has been doing. I answer as best I can. I tell her how Kim twisted my arm and took my lunch box.

Telling an adult about bullying is not tattling. When you tell someone, you are trying to protect yourself or someone else. When you tattle, you are trying to get someone else in trouble.

13

"I'm very glad you told me," Mom says. "Bullying is not OK, and it's not your fault. Tomorrow I'm going to talk to your teacher about making this better. I also know some things you can do right now that may help. Do you want to hear them?"

I nod.

Mom tells me confident kids aren't bullied as much as worried and sad kids. She says that if I keep my eyes up, my shoulders back, and my arms to my sides, I will look more sure of myself. She also tells me to try not to cry.

"I know you cry because you're scared, and you scream because you're angry. But that's just what Kim wants. It makes Kim feel powerful when you get upset."

Fighting back may seem like a good way to respond to physical bullying. But it can get the person who's bullied into as much trouble as the person who bullies. Fighting may make the bullying get even worse.

I'm not sure I can do what she's telling me.

"You're really smart, Bailey," Mom says. "I bet you have some ideas for keeping safe."

I think about how Kim picks on me when I'm alone. "I guess I could walk with other kids. And try to stay near adults."

"Great ideas." She kisses me good night. "Remember that I love you, and I'm always on your side. You're my hero."

"Like Mighty Raccoon?" I ask.

She smiles. "Better than Mighty Raccoon."

Looking someone in the eyes is one way to appear stronger. Some people find it easier to look at the bridge of someone's nose rather than directly into the eyes.

The next day at school, my stomach
twists, and I already feel like crying.
Can I do what Mom taught me?

Then I think about Mighty Raccoon, who's super
strong and in control. I imagine I'm Mighty Raccoon
and don't feel so scared.

When the lunch bell rings, I jump up and walk down the hallway with other kids. Kim leaves me alone. My lunch tastes great.

Kids who bully mostly pick on other kids when adults aren't watching. It helps to stay close to teachers or monitors in places like the lunchroom and playground, and near the driver on the school bus.

That afternoon, Mrs. Simms finds me on the playground. **"Your mom called me,"** she says. **"Bailey, I didn't know you were being bullied. If it happens again, I want you to tell me right away. You can leave early for lunch if you want to. And I'll make sure the lunch and playground monitors keep an eye on you."**

Mrs. Simms thinks I should start seeing Mr. Jones, the school counselor. She says kids who have friends aren't bullied as much as kids without friends.

Mr. Jones can help me learn how to make more friends.

Mom checks in with me a lot. She asks how I'm doing and if I'm still being bullied. Mrs. Simms says she is going to talk about bullying in class.

I'm glad I told my mom. I know I have adults and kids on my side. I don't let kids like Kim bother me as much anymore.

Glossary

bully—to frighten or pick on someone over and over

confident—to feel good about yourself

counselor—a person trained to help with problems or give advice

ignore—to not look at or listen to

monitor—a person who keeps track of people, a place, or situation; a school monitor can be a teacher, teacher's aide, or other adult who works at the school

supervise—to watch over or direct a group of people

threaten—to say you will harm someone or something in the future

Read More

Bracken, Beth. *The Little Bully.* Little Boost. North Mankato, Minn.: Picture Window Books, 2012.

Cook, Julia. *Tease Monster: A Book About Teasing vs. Bullying.* Building Relationships. Boys Town, Neb.: Boys Town Press, 2013.

Sornson, Robert. *The Juice Box Bully: Empowering Kids to Stand Up for Others.* Northville, Mich.: Ferne Press, 2010.

Internet Sites

FactHound offers a safe, fun way to find Internet sites related to this book. All of the sites on FactHound have been researched by our staff.

Here's all you do:

Visit *www.facthound.com*

Type in this code: 9781479569410

Super-cool stuff! Check out projects, games and lots more at **www.capstonekids.com**

Index

All of the books in the series: